Seeing...

Through Nature

Poetry by

Jane Mayes

authorHOUSE™
1663 Liberty Drive, Suite 200
Bloomington, Indiana 47403
(800) 839-8640
www.AuthorHouse.com

First published by AuthorHouse 08/02/05

ISBN: 1-4208-5574-3 (sc)

Library of Congress Control Number: 2005904515

Printed in the United States of America
Bloomington, Indiana

This book is printed on acid-free paper.

Cover illustration - "Shore Enough" from an original watercolor by Jane Mayes

Table of Topics

Creation	*1*
Nature	*11*
Nature's Creatures	*21*
Growing Things	*65*
Rain	*77*
Sunlight ~ Moonlight	*85*
Seasons	*97*
Eco-love	*109*
Water	*115*
Streams & Rivers	*120*
Lakes & Seas	*129*
Meet the Poet	*163*
Notes on Poems	*165*

Breathe A Poem

If you would write a poem,

see beauty in a lichen,

history in a fossil;

feel humanity's heartbeat

and hear the hum of the universe.

Inhale the scent of thunderstorm;

then exhale your poem.

Creation

Prologue

The first cell of primeval dawn
yawned sleepily, then stretched,
divided, evolved, became
mother-cell of amoeba, dinosaur,
            fish, frog and snake,
            flying avian species, and
            earth-bound mammals. We
then, interconnected through
chemical and organic ancestry,
have grown apart, forgotten
our common birth and history.

I call upon the clan-cousins:
            tell me your stories,
            teach me your lore.
Together we can journey toward
the next phase of our common evolution,
where we may become aware
of this invisible life-force-energy
            that we share.

Time Revisited

Fossil at my foot,
coelenterate from eons gone
when no man stepped
upon the sands of your time,
you trigger images
of mastodons and dinosaurs
unwittingly trampling you
into the silt of ages past.

Like the ice man
you have been frozen in time,
clue to a past
that would have been forgotten
had you not washed up here
at my feet, where before
were only horsetails
as reminders of a simpler,
purely natural time,
uncomplicated by
manipulated minerals,
mechanical monstrosities,
and the confusing profusion
of binary cyber-switches.

Suspended Animation

On this breathless morning
no leaf quivers,
        no bird call breaks
        the silent spell of dawn.
The lake mirrors attention
        as if awaiting a grand proclamation
        from a higher power.

How can the world
        be spinning this fast
        as it hurtles through space
        at such a speed,
and we not sense the rush
        of wind in our ears
and the pull of gravity?

May my life be thus:
        serene and exempt
        from the hurried tempo of life,
        the strobing media action scenes
that explode in my ears
        and shudder the foundation
        of my serenity.

Romanticide

Were I the first on earth to witness
the wonder of a sparkling night sky,
would I react with fright or rapture?
Would I suspect the cloak of evening
to be wearing thin, letting beams
of sunlight filter through?

Now in the cool light of science
we have charted the skies,
labeled each star,
measured magnitudes,
numbered distances
in light years from earth,
and determined the edge
of the universe.

The romance of the heavens
lies buried in the ancient myths
of the constellations.

Bearings

A black bear shadows me
through thickening forests.
I glimpse it intermittently,
but always sense its presence.
When I pause, it rests as well.
I try to divine its intent:
does it hunger for my scent,
bear a message of portent,
or is it merely curious?
Show yourself, Ursa Coeli,
.......Bear of Heaven.

Luna Love

What is it about the moon
that lovers yearn and rhapsodize?
The sun warms, but the moon's
blue light casts a chilly spell.
Is it that the moon,
like unrequited love,
seems unattainable,
its face bearing
that eternal, taunting grin?
But you— you are sitting here
beside me; and your warmth
penetrates my jacket's insulation
to embrace my heart
as it eclipses my soul.

Free Fall

my life is a dream
and i am in control
but somewhere
in the middle
of my well-ordered
blue-printed dream
a voice suggests
that i wake up
urges me to
WAKE UP

i awake
the voice is
the wind
screaming past
my ears
i hug myself
for protection
only to spin
in heels-over-head
gyrations
i am no help to me

i am hurtling
through space
toward what
where is the familiar
blue marble
with its swirl of white
where the thumb
of my snug mitten
nestled in the pond

arms flail
hands clutch at nothingness
grasping only air
that dissolves like
my sense of security

spreading my arms
wide to embrace
my situation
i can float
i feel in charge again
in charge of what
i hang in space
directionless
silence and blackness
are louder
than the screaming wind

turning
there is a planet
drawing me
the gravity of the situation
eludes me
i am too dense
to understand
what does it hold
the rushing air
shushes my fears
as i struggle
to accept
the purple-pink
spongy landing
a sigh of safe finality
whispers security at last

but this sphere too
is hurtling through space
around what
does my planet revolve
what the center
of its universe

Wanderlust

Sometimes on a busy day
when there's hardly time to think,
and so many tasks are on my mind
that I feel I'm on the brink,

an image of a peaceful place
will show on my mind's screen,
like a mini-mental vacation;
and I'm once again serene.

My dentist office trips
are to a high and craggy hill;
the view so elevating
overrides the drill.

When crowds and schedules pressure,
Lake Huron's vast expanse
of water mirroring the clouds
puts me in a calming trance;

and when I'm tired of the pace,
and news seems terrifying,
I sit and watch the sun set—
it's always pacifying.

So take a trip with me some time:
you'll have no bags to bring,
no need to arrange vacation time;
and it won't cost a thing.

Nature

God of Magnificence and Minutia

I see you, God, mirrored
in the grandeur of Lake Huron,
where you magnify
the power of weather
and reflect your creativity
as you artistically play
with the vast palette of the sky.

In the western red rock
peaks and pinnacles
you loom large over me;
your massive, mute presence
slowly sculpts
your majestic profile
for me to admire
in my insignificance.

But when I examine
the delicately exquisite beauty
          of a dragonfly's wing,
smell the heady perfume
          of a tiny arbutus flower,
and learn of the complex
          chemical processes
          in a single fir needle,
I know that your work
is evident in them as well,
and that you are not
          too grand or remote
to care about
          the tiniest cell
                    within me.

Conversation With Nature

I know you love me, little wren;
you trill your joy,
    your ecstasy with life,
to share with me that wonder.

Oh, larkspur,
    when I admire your beauty
with a gentle fingering
of your delicate purple petal,
you reply with a dainty pollen kiss.

Welcoming mosses,
you quietly carpet my forest walk,
offering your velvet cushion
to grateful passersby.

Dear broken spiral shell,
you expose your intricate
    inner structure
that we might recognize with awe
the work of a master architect.

Oh, lowly soil of this rich earth,
you teach the great lesson,
taking that which seems lifeless
and giving nourishment
    back to creation.

And I,
what have I to give
to demonstrate my love?
I smile joyfully,
paint a picture, write this poem
of praise and gratitude.

Don't Go

O bobolink, o cricket,
o miniscule arbutus,
if you were to disappear,
who would provide
your whimsical beauty,
your cheerful music
on a summer night,
your sweet, sensuous scent
to delight and inspire?

And you,
who would be my companion
to whimsy me when I am alone,
to hum a pleasant melody
and send me fragrant thoughts
when I need a gentle touch
and the warmth of a loving smile?

Time Zone

noon bells chime

from the mountains
wind whispers
a lonely calf bleats
a rook calls randomly
invisible birds twitter
treetops roil
            on the wooded slopes

echoing across the valley
over a verdant landscape
distant church bells
toll their response

The Furies on Spring Break

The ancient Furies scream loose
from some long-locked Pandora's box,
howling through the open corridor
under the roof of our rented condo.

In the top floor bedroom we huddle
and wonder: Will the roof fly off,
and vacuum us out of bed;
or will it collapse, burying us
under a shroud of rubble?

Now they pry loose the plexiglass dome,
slamming it against the loft wall;
they wrench off the orange awnings
and slide them across the parking lot
like shuffleboard disks.
In spite of closed windows,
single hairs of my head tremble
in the eerily moving air.

Outside our door the light globe
offers itself as a bhoodan, and crashes
several flights down the stairwell.
Power is low, but the radio crackles,
"..worst storm of the century...
...entire eastern third of the nation...
...inches of snow in Atlanta..."

Palm trees bend their backs
to the buffeting blast; their fronds
part like hair to reveal the pale scalps
of their stem heads.

Now sirens scream at the Furies.
Will they scream for us next?
We have filled pots and pans
with fresh emergency water.
I take a shower to escape the noise,
but the insistent imps taunt me
through the ventilator.

We entertain our guests at Othello,
turning the disks from black to white
and back to black, like the wavering score
between the storm and us.
By the second day, the Furies tire,
only hurling light objects, like epithets,
in our direction. As we venture out,
we step around debris, and remark
at the incongruity of icicles hanging
from tropical palmettos.

We file like geese to the theater
for diversion. We watch Bill Murray
re-live Groundhog Day—
what if this were our day to be relived
until we get it right?
As we return, light snowflakes scatter
like ghosts of cockroaches in the light.
Clutching our clothing to us,
we wend our way to the fitful beach,
where stiff bodies of whelks and starfish
lie like victims of our one-sided war.

Finally, we propose a pact:
they retreat to their box,
and we'll clean up their mess.

Night Wind

Who speaks to me in the wind-voice
which awakens me from sleep
in our cottage by the sea?

What is the message
carried on the wind?
Is it the tide that rushes
to share its secrets,
or voices from outer space?
What is its origin?

The mute wind only speaks
when it finds its voice
in the trees, or nooks
and crannies of buildings,
or the hair flowing
about my ears.

How does it expect
to be understood
when it speaks a language
composed of only vowels,
and sometimes H?

What is so important
that it interrupt
my conversation with
my dream-child?

When will it relent,
and cease its efforts
to reach our hearts
to teach its truths
to minds which think
it is only the wind?

Trespassers Will Be Prosecuted

My eyes trespassed your woods today.
It was early morning while fresh snow lay
White and still on every branch and blade.

The deer and birds had already been there
(None would have known had the ground been bare),
And left tracks as proof of intent to invade.

They were judged and imprisoned in paradise.
Oh, that the judge would try my eyes
And determine their fate by the same design;

But I was sentenced instead to carry
For life the forbidden memory
Of the Eden behind the "No Trespassing" sign.

Wired

Outdoors a cicada emits its
sizzling, piercing, high-wire song.
Half hidden by the pine tree,
the transformer on the corner
stealthily filters electricity
into our home, bringing
light, power for cooking,
warmth, sounds and visions
that electrify my senses.
News of turmoil, crimes and dissent
infiltrate my life through silent sockets
as shoulders hunch to ward off tension.

Even sequestered in the silent
darkness of my bedroom
I am enmeshed in a maze of wires
that wait to surge their response
to the commands of the next day.

Then my beloved takes my hand
and leads me along the wooded path
toward the pond's calm waters,
where water bugs skate aimlessly,
and frogs snooze with noses to the sun.
We stroll through pastures
where mares contentedly graze
as foals play foolishly at tag
with a tantalizing butterfly.

Gradually the warmth of the hand
that cups my own diffuses my tension.
Serenity and solidity ground me;
and I return to the de-electrified me.

Nature's Creatures

Silent Boarders at the Mayes B & B

We have several secret boarders
who inhabit our domain—
They pay no rent, make no noise,
and never cause us pain.
They're easy-going folks, and humble,
never make the upstairs rumble,
nor do they ask us what we think.
The only time that we're aware
is that occasional tuft of hair
left by the bunnies near their lair
under the enclosed deck stair;
or when the raccoons return to their housing
in our old oak tree after carousing
all night on the town, and they cross our lawn
furtively one hour after dawn.
You'd never know the 'possum's around—
he shuffles about with nary a sound;
and skunk stays cleverly out of sight,
just excavating for grubs at night.
He merely causes tolerable pain
when the scent of his hair spray tweaks my brain.
Those acrobatic tree-rat squirrels are kinda fun to see,
and it's flattering to have boarders so nuts about me!
We spy the deer at dusk or dawn;
and turkeys awkwardly cross our lawn.
All these are quite a thrill to see.
The only boarders that bother me
are the geese that come to nibble our grass.
Their droppings are a pain someplace.
My husband goes running in their direction
armed with a pop-gun to serve their eviction.
They flap away with a great deal of fuss,
and we are left to clean up their muss.
Then we realize as the gun goes back in the closet:
they're the only boarders who've made a deposit!

Beastly Beauty

The painted lady flaunts
    botox-injected lips,
    Cleopatra eyes,
    padded hips,
    a harlot's cheeks,
    augmented breasts.
She throws her image
        back at God, pouting,
"You should have done a better job!"

Meanwhile,
    the crow's jet feathers
        glisten with a deep blue sheen;
    'Possum's pink nose
        complements fur of gray;
    the common dandelion
        is content with merely yellow;
    and the clover attracts the bee
        with its own sweet perfume.

Oh! Possum!

Possum-pink-toes,
you waddle erratically,
snuffling amid leafy clumps
hoping for some tidbit
that your squinty eyes
might have missed.

Hearing our approaching steps,
you shuffle toward shelter
in the bramble thicket,
naively leaving star-like tracks
in the thawing snow
to openly point the way
to your secret hiding place.

The Visit

Two deer appear...
back from a former life.
As if having promised
not to reveal the secrets
from the other side of being,
they cautiously skirt the issues
at the parameters of our yard,
curiously studying my movements
as if delving for recognition.
They eye-mail a message of love
then bound over the wall
and into the foggy forest
of my incomprehension.

*　　*　　*

November deer pause-
color of dirt and stubble
hide in open field

Timing is Everything

In January
squirrels flirt precariously
on flimsy branchlets.
She teases him,
flicking her tail
tantalizingly near.
He, preoccupied with a nut,
awaits the generation
of more seminal fluid.

* * *

Bushy-tailed tree rats
playing catch-me-if-you-can
high in the treetops

Vole

As you busily scrounge and squirrel
in the tangle of my unkempt, so-called garden,
the roof of your workplace disappears
tornado-like on the tines of my rake.
You're not in Kansas, Vovo,
it's Michigan; and I'm putting my garden to bed
for the winter that you are anticipating
on your inner clock, crossing off the days
on your invisible calendar.

Trustingly you scurry into the nearest tunnel,
the tattered sleeve of my red barn jacket,
left carelessly on the grass in the heat of raking.
You should have read the red as a warning,
but the dark hole in the sun-warmed fabric
offered the false promise of safe haven.

I lift the jacket, give in to the impulse
to one-finger-pet the silky softness of your furry back,
frozen in Lilliputian terror at my feet;
then, realizing that I cannot force friendship,
step back and watch you bobble in panic
over autumn-green tufts of grass,
frantically seeking asylum.

Come back to the banquet anytime,
dear evidence of planetary survival.
The deer, rabbits, 'possums, raccoons, birds,
snakes, mice, toads, spiders and insects
will make room for one more; but please,
leave a sampling for your hostess –
it's the polite thing to do
since she shares it all with you.

Send a Ferret

Fearless, feisty ferret
insinuates her nose
into every nook and cranny
in search of the choice morsel –

no subtle sleuthing,
no crafty strategy,
just direct and to the goal,
all attention focused on the task.

The damp ground heavy
with the musky scent
sets her salivating
in eager, driven anticipation;

sniffing, nostrils twitching,
she passes over grubs and roots
to snatch her prey and drag it
struggling from its burrow.

Mission accomplished,
she cleans her blood-stained face
and preens her fur
while planning her next strike.

Can you ever
really tame a ferret
once she's tasted
blood?

Pasturations

Leggy colt
explores
sniffs at a butterfly
parries and kicks
at imaginary foes
races after a barn swallow
then with great urgency
rushes back to its mare

My spirit joins his
I am young again

* * * *

Patience

Furry foal
can't quite reach the grass to nibble,
peers from behind his mother's rump,
mare's tail draped rakishly across his face.

He tries to climb her back—
because it's there,
or maybe to see the other side.

Testing unsteady legs
he dashes away
only to dart back,
slamming into mama's flank.

Unflinching,
she looks around as if to say,
"What ARE you doing NOW?"

Everycat

Opening the door to the potting shed
the orange tabby cat merely pushed with her head,
and with an air of disgust for the fertilizer smell
and the scent of herbs that she knew so well,
that cat walked out like royalty.
As she passed, she messaged me
that she was worthy of better, and did I know
that she was accustomed to better things
like caviar and late-night flings
on the neighbor's fence?

"Oh, yes, and are you not in awe
of the dainty way I shake my paw
to rid my fur of morning dew?
And furthermore, it would seem that you
might admire me from a better place
for vantage of my fine, whiskered face.
Of course, you have come to worship me;
and it's a rightful place for you to be
since I am deserving of recompense;
            and since I AM,
            therefore you are....nothing, I sense."

Crawdad Days

Below the waterfall
at Canon's Pond dam
crayfish lurk under rocks
and eavy creek banks,
unseen by passersby
or even summer's sun.

Unable to resist
our probing sticks,
they seize the tips.
We seize the opportunity
to yank them from
their watery lairs
onto the loamy bank,
where, out of their element,
they clumsily threaten us
with menacing pincers
until we gently place them
back into the shallows
and laugh to see
how lightning-swiftly
their tails repel them,
darting backwards
into rocky havens.

Cardboard Frogs

amphibian road kill
tadpole dreams
of crossing the highway
quashed before fruition
cardboard frogs
petrifying in the sun
provide
qualms in the queasy
warnings to the weak
omens for the hesitant
foolish frogs who believe
the swamp must be more savory
across the street

Leap, Frog, Leap!

On the glassy pond
of our cocktail table
two verdigris frogs
in fluid lines
that belie their static,
acrobatic pose
are playing.

They appear sexless,
yet I know that he's
the one crouched
on the lily pad
whose stem swirls up
to form a candle cup.
Feet widely planted,
he steadies the stem
with one hand;
the other supports her foot.
Thus boosted by her mate
she climbs ever higher,
one arm around the stem,
the other waving
a grand "Ta-da-a-ah!"

Are they playing,
or are they, like moths,
inexorably drawn to the flame?
Have they pooled their efforts
to snare a bug from the flower,
or does he loyally support her
in yet another frog-a-mamie quest?
No matter; the view may be
better from the bottom.

Vulnerable

I am a naked snail,
a defenseless slug,
tentatively testing
each turn in my path
with sensitive tentacles.

Frowns. Put-downs!
Carping criticism.
Abrasive words!

Feelings bruised,
I retract my feelers
and withdraw,
wishing for
a hard shell
like real snails have.

Meanwhile
my salty tears
are dissolving
my entire being
into a froth of
nothingness.

Reptilian Response

Put yourself in my position.
Lying down here on my belly
only seeing eye-to-eye with vermin
is downright humbling and
terrifying at times.
Come down here and get
a snake's eye view of the world:
a dog, a deer, a heron from this angle
loom as monstrous threats.
Now you see why I hide
under rocks and fallen trees.
Now you understand why
I don't see the big picture,
the stunning beauty of the sunset.
Don't take my bite personally;
it's my only defense
since that apple incident.

Snake-in-the-Grass

Snake in the grass,
you crawl on your ass
with surprisingly minimal torque;

and you are one
who smells with your tongue,
which resembles a tuning fork.

Strangely enough,
it's the very same stuff,
a stick-like fork, that will trap you;

and when you tire
of your present attire,
your skin proceeds to unwrap you.

On a medical pole
or down in a hole
is where your friends can find you.

You can shimmy up
for a claret cup,
(processed from apples, mind you)

or slither down
with nary a sound,
and an attitude "never you mind";

but better beware
of that female fair
with a serpentine axe to grind!

The Strike

The serpent has slithered into paradise.
With his probing, forked tongue
he has sensed our weakness,
which is our strength, greatness
and delusion of invulnerability.
Selecting the largest eggs in the nest
he has opened his disjointed jaws
and swallowed them two at a time,
smashing the dreams of thousands
and leaving a shambled nest.

We seek him in the ruins of hope,
in the dank caves of cunning,
between the cracks of our security,
even in the cleft of our own bosom.

Call up honor, truth and justice
to trap him under the heel
that bears the weight
of a billion heavy hearts
that beat as one.

Seductive Serpent

Shall we watch
as the children
play with snakes,
brightly colored
as they are
with their charm
and sensuous grace
beguiling until
they open wide
their disjointed jaws
and swallow
them in?

One For the Birds

Why is the owl considered so wise?
It's clearly not related to size,
for birds' brains are very tiny things;
their skills are more attached to wings.

Though a parrot doesn't have visible ears,
that gossip repeats every word that it hears.
Bob White, who's known for his crisp, clear call,
blathers his color preference to all.

The loon's eerie call at twilight haunts;
and you know what sadistic whip-poor-Will wants!
There's big-mouth crow with his raucous "Caw!";
while wren's sweet trill fills us with awe.

Cuckoo is crazy over clocks,
and mockingbird just sits there and mocks.
Oh, towhee's hospitable as can be
inviting you in to "Drink-your-tea!";

but owl asks questions – that's why he's wise –
he already knows what? when? where? and why?
That leaves one question left to do;
so he's constantly asking, "Who? Who? Who-o-o?"

Demise of Reason

The dejected dove was tiring
as she flew from country to country
        between religious factions
            and among the people,
whose greedy hatred
blinded their eyes to her presence.

The ever-rejected olive branch
        became wilted and broken.
Finally, an orange-clad
        sportsman said,
"Let us shoot the dove
        for our hunting pleasure."

And now the dove is dead.
Bury her face down,
so the oily blood we are shedding
won't mix with the tears in her eyes.

Royalty Passes By

In the hushed stillness of winter,
as I stood at the window pondering
the pregnant silence of dawn,
the monarch of birds made his appearance
with broad, dark wings undulating
majestically like a royal cape flowing.
The white feathers of his head,
bright as a diadem,
supported his claim to nobility.
With his regal, hooked beak
and eyes fixed on lofty purpose,
he never deigned to turn his head
to see me standing there in awe
like a loyal subject with mouth agape.

Hawk!

The name suggests "attack!"
But when I see you gliding –
          silently, lazily, peacefully,
You point out what I lack.

My feet are magnetized,
Attached to earth like glue;
Yet for a feathered moment –
          expansively, powerfully, joyfully,
I'm up there with you!

*   *   *   *   *

poetry takes wing
to fly above our earthly
imaginations

Descant

Outside our bedroom window
in the dark of a rainy
spring midnight
a lone bird warbled
its varied love song
as if it knew what
we were doing
with our windows open.
It trilled on for an hour
in the middle of that night
singing descant
to my heart's melody.

Elegy to a Grosbeak

The rose-breasted grosbeak
lies in state on our deck
before the picture window,
laid out in black and white tuxedo
with the cerise bib.

Had it not been for his fatal accident,
he might have passed unnoticed.
New in the neighborhood,
he was unaccustomed to the dangers
of civilization.
A downy tuft and a smear of blood on the pane
provide the only clues to his demise.

Meanwhile, grackles and cowbirds,
starlings and blackbirds abound
with their raucous to-do at the feeder
and their messy table manners.
I have wished some of them dead;
but here lies beauty
with lifeless black eyes.

Bandits

Morning, sky, lake, trees
are varied tones of gray.
The breeze has not yet roused,
and only bright snow contrasts
along the frozen shoreline.

Black forms of birds clustered
at openings in the ice
draw me to the window telescope
to see a band of cormorants,
those deep-diving lake pillagers,
plotting their next raid.

Responding to some secret signal,
they rise together, join another band,
and disappear through the obscuring
veil of fog over open water.

Social Creatures

Just before sundown
geese honk a syncopated
chorus of various notes as they rise
from their afternoon rest on the lake.
They seem to consult each other
about the best flight path
to their favorite cornfield for dinner.
Once in formation, they chide
each other good-naturedly,
contentedly gabbling as they flap
their way under the clouds.

We women board our bus
for the return trip from
a pleasant theater experience.
The happy murmur of friendship
becomes a celebration of sisterhood;
dark settles, and the murmur
drowns out the drone of the motor.
As treble soprano and alto voices
of varying tempos and tones
intone thoughtful discussions,
exchange of ideas, future plans,
and memories of shared experiences,
the volume escalates, punctuated
by outbursts of laughter.

In the morning I gather eggs.
The hens in the chicken yard
cluck and chatter as they execute
their scratch-and-peck feeding dance,
contentedly secure in the sorority
of familiar fowl.

Shattered Dreams – a case to be cracked

Beside our wooded pond
a gray Canada goose lies
camouflaged on a shabby nest
of last fall's leaves now the color
of her muted feathers.
Motionless as if in death
her neck extends along the ground.

Quietly and cautiously
from across the sheltered pond
we check the nest each day
and find her in the same position
exactly as the day before.

One day only scattered leaves
and shell shards strewn in disarray
give testimony to nature's violence.
No proud goose and gander
parade their fluffy goslings –
our hopes are dashed
like the empty, mangled eggshells
strewn along the bank.
One egg remains intact,
at the pond bottom where
it lies out of reach, doomed.
Disappointment rising to anger,
we demand, "What predator
dared to risk death or mutilation
by her swift empowered beak?"

The answer to the riddle
lies in the one remaining egg
lying on the bottom of the pond.

Creatures of Night

Where do night birds go
        when it is day?
Do they follow the darkness
        far, far away,
eventually circling 'round the earth,
reveling in their midnight mirth,
knowing they've won
        the race with day?

Listen, Mockingbird

Mockingbird,
you've been maligned:
Your very name
sounds so unkind;
but some have heard
your warble sweet—
You merely mirror
those you meet.

The day I turned sixty-five
vultures circled overhead,
spoiling an otherwise glorious day.

* * *

Atop the fence post
reminding me of life's end
birthday buzzard waits

* * *

The loon surface dives
Appears where you don't expect—
A laughing trickster

* * *

Hoping for handouts
baby birds stretch wide their beaks
for succulent worms

Intimate With Insects

To think I almost brushed you away
from the table top where you lay
among bits of fallen pollen
from yesterday's bouquet!

The iridescent yellow of your wings,
transparent robe suitable for kings,
drew me to a closer look
at this tiniest of things.

Magnifying glass drew you nearer—
made exquisite beauty clearer,
brought realization
making your value dearer.

Miniscule body delicately made
in the palest green alluring shade,
only two black dots for eyes
gave substance weighed.

What else exists beyond our sight
that hasn't yet been brought to light?
More evidence of nature's
miniaturization of delight.

Scope

The ant sees the grain of pollen,
the bit of leaf that lies
within the inch-high stratum
of its world. It sees
what it needs to know
for gathering food,
for self-preservation.

Meanwhile, I want
to perceive the larger picture,
see beyond the universe
through the eye of God.
But could my finite brain
and fragile human heart
survive such knowledge?

To Be Or Not To Bee

Do little bees learn

    at the queen bee's knees

about preparing

    for winter's freeze?

They work all summer

    to save up honey;

this honey-bee "gold"

    is worth more than money.

They're buzzin' and hummin'

    and making it sweet,

so we can enjoy

    our breakfast treat.

Centipede's Secret

Centipede, you are a fraud!
All these years I've ooh'd and ah'd,
marvelled at your form and grace
slithering from place to place
under leaves and boards and rocks,
behind the purple hollyhocks,
into our basement to find a treat,
each foot marching to a different beat.
Now at last I know the reason
why you hide in every season:
so no one will find out, indeed—
you're an OCTO-DEKA-HEXA-PEDE!

Razzle Dazzle

Oh, emerald bug on filament legs,
you land briefly on my sunlit arm,
vainly turn a proud pirouette
to allow me to fully admire
your stunning beauty before
the music of a breeze lures you on
to more prestigious runways.

Musca Domestica

Befuzzed, black housefly,
you settle on the counter top
to siphon up a drop of milk.
Contentedly full, you preen
your face with agile forelegs
like a loan shark
rubbing his hands in gleeful
anticipation of excessive interest;
but I know your real interest lies
in a piece of putrid meat
or an attractive bit of shit.

Regrets Only

Mrs. Tabanus Atratus, giant horse fly,
you landed much too near my sunning legs.
Being familiar with the triangle scar of your bite
        and the spurt of blood you draw
        when dowsing for arteries,
my impulse snapped you with a towel.
Now your compound eyes stare
at hundreds of nothings, sightless;
and as you lie with legs upraised,
it is too late to beg your pardon.

Territorial Dispute

Black beetle with flimsy antennae,
    you land on my clipboard. Surprised,
you shyly crawl to the underside
    seeking safety and anonymity;
but I turn it over and expose you again.
Reflexively I flick you away,
    without knowing why.
We study each other where you land.
Who will flinch first?
Curiosity draws me nearer
    to count your legs, and
finding only five, I am filled with guilt
    until I see you crawl away
    quite adroitly. But now you circle 'round
and crawl up the back leg of my chair.
Are you bent on revenge,
    or merely reclaiming your home
that I mistakenly thought was my chair?

Starring Role

Gray grasshopper, the color
of our weather-beaten deck,
wants to be in a poem.
He lands on a knot in the wood
as if in a spotlight center stage
and stares me down and up.
Convinced in his tiny brain
that he has negotiated a contract,
he spreads his cream-edged cape
to illustrate his aerial talents.
When I quit writing, he circles back
to see how the project's progressing.

Okay, okay, Your Grayness,
you're memorialized. Now leave
your tiny autograph and fly away.

If You Believe in Crickets, Rub Your Legs Together

Alone
in my campus basement apartment
without husband, children, or pets.
Alone – and feeling intimidated
by raucous men across the hall
behind the ever-open door marked
with mysterious, secret symbols,

I stock the food my family wouldn't eat,
make three day's worth of one-dish ratatouille,
and study until early morning.
As sleep sifts around me,
Bigfoot returns to the room above,
thumping across my ceiling for hours,
leaving me sleep-deprived –

and alone.

One evening a cricket chirps a bid
to sublet my lonely domain.
I must evict him (like the previous owner's pet
excrement that lay dehydrated in the closet).
On hands and knees I prowl the premises
and find innocent beady eyes peering out
from makeshift hearth under the stove.

We strike a deal:
I will pay him in lettuce-leaf lucre;
henceforth he will be My Cricket.
He will tolerate my ruminant monologues,
sing me soothingly to sleep at night,
and leave my cotton clothing
alone.

Lady ? Bug

Ladybug, you fly to me
like a bittersweet berry
blown by the autumn breeze.
But what is your mission?
Never turning your head,
you hunch along on my hand,
a bug with a purpose;
yet I never actually see you
decimating the aphid population
as your press agent claims.
I have even set you down
in a succulent ladybug paradise,
in the midst of a horde
of transparent aphids
teeming on my rose buds.
You blindly crawl over them
in your pretense of having
more important things to do
elsewhere. Your attention
to your "mission" is a ruse,
and now I even suspect
that you are no lady.

Yellow Bug Boogie

Got up this morning,
pulled on my pants,
shuffled to the bathroom,
my brain in a trance;
turned on the light
and what did I see?
A yellow bug on the sink
waving at me.

He said, "Hey there, sleepy!"
(and he giggled with glee)
"Put down that toothbrush
and dance with me!"
So we danced like Hawaii
and we danced up a tune;
and before we knew it,
it was almost noon!

Our eight feet were tapping
doing steps galore
until they just couldn't
dance any more.
I asked, "Why so happy?
What's the score?"
He said, "My wife laid a thousand eggs
under your floor!"

"If each one hatches
and THEY do the same,
there'll be a thousand thousand more
that'll have my name.
That's a million yellow bugs
looking just like me!"
He threw his hat in the air
and he shouted, "Whoooo-pee!"

Oh, NO! Woe is me!

Flutter By, Butterfly!
(A finger-play verse)

Hello, butterfly!
        Flutter by me.
Flutter closer so I can see
how colorful your wings can be.

Now land a while so we can play;
and when you can no longer stay,
I'll hook my thumbs,
        and we'll fly away!

We'll flutter about
        for hours and hours,
visit the purple and yellow flowers,
play hide and seek
        with the April showers;

and when we're tired
and we need a nap,
we'll fold our wings
and sleep on gramma's lap.

There's a Lesson Here Somewhere

Behold the butterflies
that flit and flutter
in the ethereal
ephemerality of air
carried on the currents
wafted hither
flitting among the flowers
Lo on the statice
there land four unbeforeseen
winged beauties
Eager to identify
I flit through pages
looking for lepidoptera seeking
names for new-found friends
There on the page is a photo
of the very creature orange
with black spots and vice versa
with an almost-swallowtail
but not really and a fuzzy
brown body that has dusted
the wing base with brown
They are "commas"

Something tells me,
oh, yes, I, get, the, message,
people, don't, want, to, read,
a, poem, with, no, punctuation,
commas, help, make, the, meaning,
clear.

What Birds Don't Know

Birds don't know
    when someone living here is sick.
    They chatter at the feeder
        and sit upon the sticks
    that kids have poked into the fence.

Robins don't know
    that mean folks own that home.
    They do their worm-dance in their yard
    and feed their hatchlings near the dome
    unconcerned with evil thoughts.

Eagles don't know
    who's lost in the woods.
    They soar about all unconcerned
    that in their neighborhood
    there's someone in distress.

The wren outside my window doesn't have a clue
    that tears that I was crying
    are mysteriously drying
    as the beauty of her song
    calls forth the sun.

But motherly Nature seems to know—
    She sends their flying flash of art
    and directs their varied choruses
    to delight the earthbound populace
    and heal the human heart.

Growing Things

Tenacious Tree

Through the greenery
of the forest floor
bones of a dead tree,
bark-stripped by weather,
reach up like a grasping
hand from the grave
trying to reclaim life.

Just When You Think It's Over

A dry leaf skitters across my path
like a small bird drunk on fermented berries.
It has no itinerary, no baggage to slow its passage,
no destination in mind, no quest to carry out.
Its life purpose fulfilled, it has been discarded;
yet for a moment, its bright colors
bring delight to those it briefly passes.

*   *   *   *   *   *

Wind howls above me
blowing leaves and pine needles
November folly

Celebration

The last hurrah of summer
celebrates as aspens let fall
a shower of sun-gold confetti
for a root-blanket of memory
to warm through winter's chill.

Treedium

hordes of leaves
just hanging out
photosynthesizing
day in – day out
playing parasol
to shield the birds from sun
waiting for a breeze
to rustle up some fun

* * * * *

dark green and lacy
hemlock boughs spread over me
angel wing shadows

So With Life

If you only put a raspberry into your mouth
and do not crush it, releasing
the delectable flavor that is raspberry,
you cannot know the delightful taste
that could bathe your tongue in sweetness;
but if you chew too enthusiastically,
crushing the seeds, you'll learn the meaning
of "taking the bitter with the sweet."
And with a kiwi – if you only lick its fuzzy coat,
you never get inside to discover that tangy treat.

Here's an open invitation to the fruit-timid:
Plunge right into that juicy nectar,
and you'll understand why butterflies flutter,
hummingbirds hover, and bees hum so happily.
So with life…
Dive in!

Plum Good

Is there anything better
than a plum
when the soft, sweet juices
run sensually
down your chin
and between your fingers
caressingly,
leaving a passionately
purple stain
for all to see
and know what
you've been up to?

Scent of Love

Love is the sweet scent
    of God's breath on the world—
    headier than hyacinth
    boldly declaring its ardor,
    gentler than arbutus
    hidden 'neath last fall's leaves,
        too shy to speak.
Oh, envelope me
    in the blissful perfume of love!
    Let it permeate all I encounter
        on my way.

Love's Yellow Rose

The rose is over-bloomed
and faded cream, no longer yellow.
Look closer, you can see
its gentle imperfections:
an insect mark, crippled petal,
failed symbol of a fruitful season.

Though life scars lives
and mars with changes all,
love endures, remains unbroken,
a never-fading flower
beyond the reach of time
and place.

Between the Cracks

In the arid gravel
along preoccupied sidewalks
among castoff cigarette butts
and broken bits of life's chaff,
which provide neither nourishment,
                    nor encouragement,
                    nor reason for existence,
          out of sheer persistence
          there survives, even thrives
          great beauty.

Some call them wild carrots
          for their tap roots that auger
          deep in search of moisture;
but others, captivated by the intricacy
          of the delicate, white, lacy flowers,
          know this regal European beauty
                    as Queen Anne's Lace.
The queen's blue sailor came along
          to flavor her coffee and simply serve:
          endive-leafed chicory hovers nearby
          with cerulean flowers whose heavenly hue
          belies their stem's toughness.
He nor the queen will ever be seen
          drooping. Bravely they try
          to hold their heads high;
          and should you attempt to remove them,
          their tenacious roots
                    and rope-strong stems
                    will prove you a fool.

Between the cracks of slum playgrounds,
          beside shadowed doorways,
          amid covert conditions,
          in spite of neglect
          and poor treatment by man,
                    these beautiful children survive.

Purpose

We are seeds of varying potential,
all basking in the same light source
which falls on each one differently.

Some will spring like ivy, struggling
to reach the sky, sending tendrils
of praise heavenward. Others creep

along the ground, providing cover
in a loving attempt to preserve the earth.
Some bear fruitful nourishment,

selflessly sustaining other life;
for others beauty is enough.
All are necessary to wholeness.

*   *   *   *

Sun(flower) rising
bearing seeds of tomorrow
to push clouds away

Sacred Ground

Surely this is a holy place:
house built on rock
where Indians must have stood,
arms raised to Great Spirit
as they sensed a response
in the powerful waves
that crash against the shore.

Even now the trees praise God,
branches raised in awe,
giving up their being
to the purpose of the universe.
Birds and shuffling animals
go about the business of survival
as do we, but meanwhile
I feel the holiness of this place
where the breath of that same
Great Spirit encircles our home.

Rain

Cloud Soup

Come, taste my cloud soup…
it's thinner than porridge,
but thicker than broth,
heated by lightning,
stirred by the wind
and peppered with
a modicum of zesty thunder.

Yes, it is somewhat gray,
so just close your eyes
when you tip back your head
to catch my cloud soup
as it rains on your tongue.

/ / / /

/ R / A / I / N /

/ / / / /

/
/ dewy moisture
refreshes and restores
the parched soil of my soul
withered for want of water /

/ /
/ / drops mingle
with salty tears
to follow the furrows
down my face
and wash away the pain / /

/ / /
/ / / playful pellets
pelt and sting my skin
waking me to the rainbow
spectrum of delight in living / / /

/ / / /
/ / / / gushing torrents
cascade over me
cleansing and bearing me
along life's current
to the ultimate ocean / / / /

/ / / / / / / / / / /

Floating in the Rain

The morning's not unpleasant,
        though breezy and gray
as I swim lazy laps
        in the condo pool.
A little mist won't deter me-
        I'm wet anyway.

Rolling over for a rest,
        I float for a while,
hands behind my head
        and ankles crossed,
body rising and falling
        with my breathing.

Mesmerized by the cloud cover
        reinventing its hazy pattern
and the wind parting the fronds
        of the palms reaching upward,
I lie in pure enjoyment
        buoyed up by the water.

Mist develops
        into friendly, steady raindrops
which make pock-marks on the pool
        then bounce up before sinking.
They pelt my face playfully,
        tickling elbows and knees
like chilly fairy fingers
        drumming lightly on my skin.

Garden in the Rain

Basking in the sunshine of celebration
we sipped our scented tea,
        savored the flavors of friendship,
        shared stories and ideas.
We passed around photo-memories
        of a grand European tour:
        beautiful buildings,
        impressive vistas,
        grandly groomed gardens
        of England, France, Switzerland, Italy.

Here at Eagle Bay, Michigan
        thunder rumbled,
and the artistry of rain and lightning
enriched the green of trees and grass.
Looking out the open door,
        I saw the garden,
        vivid with clean whites,
        yellows and rich purples,
smelled the freshness of the perfumed air.

Could the Luxembourg Gardens in Paris
        be more beautiful
        than these shastas and hostas
dancing to the soothing rhythm of the rain
on this pleasant summer day
right here at Eagle Bay?

Puddles

There's a whole other world
down there
        on the underside
        of puddles.

Fearing bold intrusion,
I peer shyly from the edge.
I can only guess at what goes on
in that silent, upside-down world.

Most kids jump
        into puddles with both feet.
        I never do.
I can see that the puddles are
deeper than I am tall,
and I might never be able
to return from that other world.

Arc of the Covenant

The rainbow is actually a full circle:
the visible arc offers praise to the sky;
the other half of this wedding ring
encircles the world in love.

* * * * * *

The Rainbow

In a rite between ethereal sky and lusty earth
clouds consecrate the nuptial bands
with sprinkled drops of holy water.
The sun directs a choir of colors,
which hover in visual harmony
as thunder rumbles a bass "Amen!"
in witness of the union of all life
in the presence of the power of the universe.

Elation

O world,
hold me in this day forever—
to celebrate
        the sunshine in my heart,
        the multi-colored pleasures of nature,
and delight in the company of my beloved!

Sunlight

Moonlight

Clean Slate

Night erases

the blackboard of yesterday

in preparation for

the sunrise drawing

of a brand new tomorrow.

Daybirth

A pink and blue
newborn morning
cautiously opens its eyes
at the eastern lake horizon.

Infant dawn
timidly dips her toes in
shimmering baptismal waters
as first rays of light
brashly proclaim
the arrival of a new day
amid gold and crimson
squeals of delight.

Abduction

I stole the sunrise
from the beach horizon,
furtively smuggled it home
in an abalone shell.

Its pearlescent light
shimmers on azure water
tinged delicately
with blushing magenta
and touched with tints
of aqua-green that artists
cannot duplicate.

Now I hold it captive
on my land-locked bedside table,
to admire my prize
when days are gray and dull
and the sun forgets to rise.

Shadow Child

Morning and evening shadows
are venturesome, wild, unruly.
Bent on escape, they tease me
with daring, mutinous threats,
like taunting, runaway children!

At noon, my shadow's tethered
and firmly underfoot.
It's close to me
where it should be,
and I am in control!

Dayquench

Lady sun, enticed by the clouds
over the Great Lake horizon,
dances dangerously on the edge,
then slips over the waterfall of day.
Strands of her flowing, yellow hair
slither out of the darkening woods,
then glow golden as they slide
across the surface of the lake,
and cascade after her
in a glorious glissade,
leaving only the multicolored
echo of her mute scream.

Twilight

Crimson-lined clouds become

hazy wisps of leftover day

that float in a fading sky

above a silver-frosted lake.

Trees give up their green

to be cloaked in mystery,

and shadows mask the day's secrets.

The lavender glow of a fading sunset

illuminates graying memories

that surface on waves of meaning,

and life becomes a stark silhouette

outlined against the twilight sky

without the distraction of detail

that sunlight boldly discloses.

Chromatose

As I sit by the window
of our cottage by the lake,
twilight settles into night
and trees are silhouetted
against a fading sky.
Fleeting flecks of sunlight
skitter across lambent waves
to hide behind the drapes of night
as the setting sun drains color
from a lackluster earth enrobed
in mourning shades of black and gray.

Cinereous Scenario

The wind pauses, breathless.
Ashen sky settles
on a silver lake that laps gently
at gray sandstone promontory.
Charcoal-gray trunks
of determined trees
send faded finger-roots
probing inquisitively
into shaded crevices
in gray rock.

Neither peak nor valley,
this evening stirs not my soul
with bright urgings nor deterrents;
it lulls me into reverie to delve into
the shadowed crannies of life
for answers which would scurry
from day brightness
or be obscured by darkness.

Womb of Time

The night wind
pulsed in the trees,
which swept the clouds
from the sky
to reveal a myriad
of glinting stars
and a pregnant moon
that swaddled the earth
with the white gown of
anticipation.

MIDNIGHT RITE

Strums of a distant banjo
filter through dark forest's depth
drawing me, mesmerized
by its incantation.

Carefully, stealthily
I tread the unfamiliar, loamy path
that beckons me
toward mystical sensation.

Deeper in the midnight woods
toward sounds no longer muffled,
in campfire glow tree shadows sway
like ancient dancers shuffled.

Now golden spaces brighten
between black, skeletal trees
as music draws me in
toward mellow fire.

Crisp stars, flickering blaze,
heart's subtle drumbeat
in this singular moment
collaborate to inspire.

Wrapped in rapturous aura
of the spell of song this night
I am one with haunting banjo,
warmed by love and light.

Springtime snowflakes float
like white dandelion fluff
blown by April's kiss.

* * * * * * * *

crocus appearance
signals the timid tulip
springtime has arrived

* * * * * * * *

Spring rain on wheat field
sea gulls squabble over worms
wiggly spaghetti

Seasons

Spring Fever

fresh and clean
new green
on every branch and plot
cells a-poppin'
bunnies hoppin'
birdies sing in polyglot

nests a-building
lilies gilding
poets and lovers to inspire
hearts go crazy
with every daisy
that pushes through the mire

Cycle of Life

Reverently tread the spongy terrain
on the path through springtime,
absorbing the fecundity of earth
with an awareness of all possibility
that lies within our imaginings.
The seeds of thought that wait
for germination and nourishment
swell with urgency.
Unable to restrain their power,
they blossom forth in exuberance
with a grand, perfumed "aha!"
of discovery and awareness.
Then fruition, which is discovered
beneath the bitter rind of sacrifice,
satiates the soul's appetite
with the delectable taste
of the promise of new life.

Domino Effect

Along the fence row blossoms blend
        their perfumed combinations
of wild rose, phlox and cherry blooms
        that drug me with elation.
Ah, Spring produces heady scents
        that whet the brain's sensations
and send aromatic signals
        to cause heart palpitations,
which serve to fuel the mind
        with aroused imagination
and to excite the libido
        with erotic machinations.

Fecundity

There is such beauty
in a freshly-plowed field!
After frigid dormancy,
dark, fertile soil
tantalizes the imagination
with portents of promise.
Pungent odor of loam,
moist and rich with possibility,
scents the air with a foretaste
of summer's lush growth.

Finger-like furrows
extend a caress
before converging in the distance.
Mother Earth, wooed
by the seductive invitation
whispered by the rain,
is open to receive
seeds of the future
to be incubated
by the warmth of the sun.

Entranced, we stand in wait,
anticipating the recurrence
of the miracle of new life.

Love Blooms

Spring rains must water winter's seeds of love
lying dormant until warmed by sun above;
then incubated by its radiant glow,
expansively they swell and start to grow.

When they emerge and let themselves be seen,
the summer sprouts take on a deeper green
accenting veins and blemishes and such.
There's music in the rustle of their touch.

As knowledge and acceptance blossom forth
the heady scent of romance fills the earth,
and hearty blooms proclaim their troth aloud,
rejoicing that such wonders are allowed.

Now autumn celebrates with colors fair
and showers of confetti everywhere.

Challenge

Give me wind; send me snow—

daring, drifting, swirling snow!

Push my coat between my legs

and slide me

down the hill!

Spin me dizzy in your swirlwind;

snap my scarf, you gusty tease,

with a crackling, ice-storm chill.

Barrel down upon me, juggernaut roaring with desire,

and scream your hoyden laughter

through the trees.

Tumble me along with wild abandon,

if you please;

and afterward I'll toast you, winter, warmly by the fire.

Feather-Bits

Angels shake their fluffy wings
        and feather-bits float down,
settling on the cedar trees
        and powdering the ground.

Feather-bits land on my nose
        and tickle past my ear.
When I see their feathers fall,
        I know they must be near.

So bundle up with mitts and boots,
        for it's outside we go
to make foot-patterns in the yard
        and angels in the snow.

*   *   *   *   *   *   *

Snow Growth

Last night snow bushes
sprouted from the ground;
and this morning when I awoke,
millions of tiny snow fairies
were trying to stomp them down
as they defiantly continued to grow
and spread and pile up like Tribbles.

Ageless Beauty

Overnight
hoarfrost turned the world gray;
silver-haired trees
glinted in the morning rays
in thoughtful stillness
        and serenity.

Awed
by its spectacular beauty,
we waited breathlessly
to garner its wisdom.

*   *   *   *   *   *   *

An arrow of geese
propelled by threat of winter
toward southern target

*   *   *   *   *   *   *

Seven silver swans
gracefully play crack-the-whip
in December skies

Snow Globe

On this blustery, winter day
I am the figure in a snow globe.
Aimlessly tossed by the wind
and pulled by updrafts
snow swirls around my tiny house;
like popcorn in an air machine
flakes fly in all directions.
In the meantime,
peering through the glass
I am dizzily giddy.

*   *   *   *   *   *

winter's chill attacks-
snow swirls around the cottage
barricading doors

Quiescence

From far out on the winter lake
the majestic shoreline trees
appear as lowly tundra mosses.
I seem to be the only creature
in a frozen, barren land.

The only sound is the salvo
of an ice fissure shooting into the distance,
its report tracing the crack
as far as the horizon—
then absolute silence.

The life of the blue-green water
is quelled by ice and snow,
dulled by the insipid winter sky.
The snowscape extends toward infinity;
yet a powerful presence surrounds me.

---WARNING---

My world, the sky,

are breathtaking today—

Tether me to earth,

or I shall float away!

STARSHINE

Dear other-person-who-can't-sleep

out beyond the sky so deep:

Are we just a dot to you,

in a sky of darkened hue?

Eco-love

Succor

Earth, wrinkled and parched,
thirstily extends dry cracks
as if begging for blessing.

Clouds, pregnant and gray,
heavily await their time
to deliver rain.

World, wounded by wars,
abuse and exploitation,
looks for redemption.

Spirit, hovering,
offers humanity hope
through loving selflessness.

Affluence Spoken Here

The gilded serpent

slithers over the bridge into Paradise,

lured by the landscaped luxury of manicured medians,

past impressive façades of over-scaled mansions

no longer noticed by satiated eyes.

Nature has been golf-clubbed to death

and the fruits of her seas sacrificed on altars

incensed with the smoke of burning money.

Coiling smugly,

he basks in the golden glow.

Then Would We?

"One has..through science, eyes with which it behooves us
to pay attention." - Hildegard of Bingen, 12th century

If the stars were to sear us by night,
and the sun were to scorch by day
shriveling the earth's flora,
and causing its fauna
to shed feathers and fur,
and if our own eyelids dried up
leaving us with withered stares
and crackling, parched vision,
then would we do everything possible
to heal and restore the ozone layer?
Or would we tunnel underground
leaving the soil to suffer its lonely plight
as we gnaw the remains of dead tubers,
and seek life-giving moisture
by licking damp rocks?

Beholden

From far out on the Great Lake or viewed from the air
you become aware that even the tallest trees occupy
a very small percentage of the bio-supportable space
surrounding this planet. Oh, I've read
of the miniscule portion of the atmosphere
allotted to trees, plants and us animals;
and those trees have to osmose, chlorophate,
and transpire at a pretty good rate
to replace all the oxygen that the people
and other animals use up. So it seems to me
that we should not only plant a tree on arbor day,
and hug a tree when the notion strikes,
but be begging its pardon when your string mower
clips its bark a bit, be sending mighty
positive e.s.p. thoughts of gratitude on a regular basis,
and be holding them in highest regard,
whether their leaves are hard at work
or they're standing there naked and weary;
because, if you think about it, we are servants
of the trees, they being so much bigger
than we are, and we being so hooked
on their cast-off oxygen. And as good servants,
we shouldn't have to be asked or told
what needs to be done for our master trees –
we should just do it, whatever.

Unquenchable Ember

Long after this body
is mercilessly cold
the voice will still
cry out mutely,
as in a nightmare,
to save the world
from extinction;
the retinas
will retain the imprint
of the beauty
of aurora borealis
in a star-filled sky;
and a small ember
deep in a chamber
of my heart
will continue to glow
with love for all creation.

Water

Water is so much more than the chemical formula of two hydrogen molecules combined with one of oxygen (H20). Not only is it the greatest part of our body's composition, but it is one of the essential elements supporting life on this planet.

It can be an annoyance when it appears in an inappropriate place, or it can be a life-threatening disaster in its power and magnitude, as it has the ability to quench life as well as support it. Yet water in its various personae, whether contained in a glass, pool, fountain, pond, brook, lake, or ocean, can be not only life-sustaining, but a venue for sports and recreation, an inspiration for artists, an awesome symbol for mystics as well as a therapeutic comfort for those with troubled spirits.

The poems in this section were inspired by water.

Dive right in!

Rune

Crystal waters spring forth
from the depths of the earth—
invisible ink that pens
the secret story of life.

* * * * * *

fields draining Spring rain
rivulets become torrents
rushing to the lake

Filtration

Like water

straining through sand,

our lives flow

downward

through time.

Grains of experience

filter out

our imperfections

as we learn

and release our mistakes

to the past,

then ascend, purified,

from the ultimate,

mystical well-spring

of rebirth.

The Source

Visit the well-spring of energy,
the ultimate source of all good.
Though the surface seems calm,
a constant surging and roiling,
from depths none can plumb
offers essential, pure water
to refresh the spirits,
inspire the minds,
and slake the thirsts
of those who kneel
and drink
freely.

Droplet

On a leaf tip hangs
a single drop
of water, transparent
contraposition
of the entire world
contained within
a suspended bat's eye view
of the Doppelganger
of all creation,
like a miniature photo
through a fish-eye lens
that captures an entire horizon.

Join the djinn within
through a skewed, square,
reflective door of light.
Is all that seems to be
compact reflection
reality encased:
gases, minerals,
flora and fauna
suspended interdependently?

Like a swelling seed
aching to burst forth
into actualization,
the essence and potential
of all reality
seem to lie dormant
in
this
s i n g l e
drop.

BROOKING THE TRUTH

I

How charming the brook
as it babbles and bubbles along!

Its varied voices
bear me, enchanted, now on its crest,
now swirling into the vortex.

Listen.

II

Glassy sheet of crystal
reflecting the muted colors of a winter day,
slithering sensually over rocks and logs,
smoothly surging, urging,
recklessly abandoning the natal spring
and rivulet nursery
to join in the grand journey
to swelling streams and unknown rivers.

...Here and again a widening bank provides respite
from the rush and tumble, the urgent surging.
Draw aside and dally a while...

The ocean's siren beckons inescapably;
the brook knows it cannot,
will not go back.

III

Aerily flowing over obstacles

designed to snare a less determined sprite,

watery torrents pommel a pool in a sandy bed.

From the depths of the indentation

spring bubbles of inspiration

ascending effervescently until set free

to the applause of surface tension.

IV

A rivulet joins the brook,
only a trickle over sodden leaves on spongy humus.

Backtrack to its genesis;
find the cause of the watery hullabaloo.

Ear to the ground, eavesdrop on secrets
gurgling under roots and rotted leaves.

Delve into the intrigue of the mystery.

Ponder the source.

V

Motto: ONWARD and DOWNWARD!

Obstacles to be overcome
challenges to be met
records to be broken –
weighing not
opportunities lost,
mistakes mishandled –
the solution lies around the next bend
... or maybe never.

VI

Mo
lec
ular
unity.
Tight little
band of droplets
forcing their will
on leafy, rooted bank,
undermining the
unsuspecting
hemlocks.

Some, overcome
with giddiness of mob rule,
splash free, only to perish
on the dry
bank.
In
unity
there is
daring, intense
mountain-moving
force. In unity there
is more unity.
****

VII

A picture is worth a thousand words,
but an infinity of words
wouldn't capture a brook.
Start with active, bouncing, churning;
add flexiful, crammeling, funambulant;
continue with vitality, zestful, and willy-nilly;
and still you can't picture it all.
A word, a photograph, a memory
may foster partial comprehension,
but you have to be there to experience brookness.

Pay Dirt

Pan life's stream
        for dust of golden talents,
        glints of miniscule insights;
collect them furtively,
        amazed at their discovery;
wash away the chaff of error
        like grains of sand
that polish the gold and serve
        to brighten understanding.
Finally, assay the hoarded collection
        and spend it all
        to further your life's work.

Mirror of Life

There is something about a stream
that beckons in passing,
invites us to follow
its wandering, watery path
into the unexplored beyond.
Its movement mirrors life
as well as does reflection.
The brook's gentle gurgling
invited us in youth to discover
nature's small marvels
in random, unexpected ways
during those endless hours
of carefree childhood.
Rushing, noisy shallows
carry us speedily to maturity
with bruising boulders
and tree-branch snags
as lessons learned.
Reflexes sharpen as we respond
to crashing warning sounds
of impending waterfalls.
Thoughts deepen with the creek
as it calls us to rest in the backwaters
and ponder the mysteries that lie
beneath sensual awareness.
Flowing through the forest,
seeking respite from the heat of summer,
we are finally enveloped soothingly
in the cool veil of mist that rises
to escort us toward the unfolding of
the Great Mystery around the next bend.

Sanctuary

Deep in the forest
dark green, lacy hemlock boughs
hover high above
summer's repelling heat.
Beneath the hushed temple dome
stillness is broken only
by the brook playing
its rocky water carillon
to summon the silent worshipers.
Mist hovers like incense haze
as we process in awe over
the damp, mossy carpet
of this natural shrine.

Current Events

Here, cross-legged on a boulder
in the middle of the river of life,
peering upstream
I try to fathom the future
as its unrelenting waters
flow onward ever toward me;
but all that lies beneath the surface
remains a mystery, for I am blinded
by glinting sunbeams and distracted
by reflections that will not penetrate.

Meanwhile, bits of flotsam
from my past tumble downstream,
sometimes resurfacing as memory,
or dredged up by those
who value such treasures
in an attempt to keep my past alive
for all to see and reconsider.

The surging waters of the present
deafen me to signs of what may come
as they crash and swirl around the security
of my sitting rock, threatening
to erode the river bed beneath;
and the chill of spray on my face
distracts me from awareness
of past or future, which meld here,
midstream in the current.

River of Life

My life is a river flowing,
flowing ever onward
toward the inevitable sea,
unseen and unexplored.
It's a long time
I've been flowing
and ever onward going
o'er adventurous terrain
in wind and sun and storm
and rich, augmenting rain.
Each bend presents a vista fresh
with boulders to delay
my progress and divert
attention to my way;
and soon the crashing roar
of the waterfall ahead
signals of impending
unknown dangers that I dread.
Will the sea be friendly
and finally bring rest, or
will there be another current
with yet another test?

Paper, Scissors, Rock

Children play the game
with hand configurations
that determine who's the winner.
They know that scissors cut through paper,
that mighty rock will smash the scissors;
and paper, though fragile, covers rock.

But the game omits even more powerful
water-- sustainer, cleanser, destroyer--
for this elusive, fluid chameleon
turns paper to sop, rusts scissors,
and, given time, can pulverize the rock.

A child believes rock to be immutable;
yet after years of current, wave and ice
the rock erodes, splits and shifts,
changing the expression on its aging face,
and morphing "Twin Sister" rocks
into quadruplets.

Great Lake-of-Two-Faces

"Red sky at night—sailors' delight;
red sky at morning—sailors take warning."
- seamen's weather axiom

Two hydrogens plus one oxygen
seem a simple formula,
but multiplied they become
a force that can erode rock,
reconfigure a shoreline,
or generate enough electricity
to power a city.

In its amniotic fluid
this lake can nurture life lovingly,
or on its surface lightly bear
an insect, bird or ship; but
in the company of an angry wind
its mood can turn and violently
bash an unwary sailor to death
upon the rocky shore.

I have seen this Great Lake,
cat-like, toss its prey about,
and toy with its victim; then,
when it tires of the game,
spit the lifeless, blue body
onto the beach.

Fog

From the harbor
the fog horn's warning
calls us to abandon
our outline for busyness.
Fog offers its cloak
of introspection,
a cool shield from
that blinding, yellow eye,
a blank, white page
for the imagination
to inscribe its details.

* * * * *

waves whisper to beach
speaking in soft sibilants
soothing lullaby

Chilly November
Lake Huron undulates like
iridescent silk

*   *   *

wavelets lick the shore
slurping its savory sand
tasting happiness

*   *   *

current caresses
waves carry me on their crest
liquid ecstasy

*   *   *

weary from long flight
honking geese snugly nestle
on mother lake's lap

Breathing

This morning by the great lake
I awoke to the sound
of my own breathing, amplified.
It came from outside my body
and eerily matched the tempo
of my own respiration.
It shusshhhed
with each exhalation,
then paused as I inhaled,
only to repeat the gentle mimicry.

I became one with the rhythm
of the waves as they caressed
the sands of the shore—
one with that vast body.
Joining in the dance of the planets,
my spirit circled space
among the galaxies.

Sweetwater Symphony

Flute notes fly up
like flocks of birds
that dip in unison,
showing dark backs, then
flashing bright under-wings.

Let violin bows
count the cadence
of swooping gulls' wings
before they settle,
bobbing on the waves.

Hear cello and viola
gronk rhythmically
with a flock of geese
as they fan the fog
with syncopated wings.

The oboe's wail floats
like a great heron
in direct, slow-motion flight,
oblivious to anything
but its destination.

The intermittent sound
of the woodwind surfaces
like a loon that dives,
only to reappear
where you least expect it.

Now a tuba groans
the final moan
of an ancient ship
swallowed into the belly
of great Lake Huron.

A cymbal finale
crashes with the breakers,
whose reverberations ebb
with the receding waves
and filter into the sand.

The Seeker

I am like a duck surface-swimming
with my head underwater seeking,
eagerly searching for nourishment
in morsels of food and darting minnows
hidden from those who peer from above,
where reflections of the sun
blind them to what lies below.
Occasionally I emerge
to scan my surroundings
for potential threats of danger,
then return to seek truths hidden
among the weeds of distraction
that lie at the bottom of awareness,
to be discovered by those who delve
deeply into life's hidden mysteries.

Shadows of Dawn

I walked the long shadows of dawn by the sea
as my love lay lingering, still dreaming for me,
and the waves played the background for music so sweet
while my heart and my feet syncopated the beat.

Birds large and small thronged the rim of the shore
preening and readying for fishing galore.
I walked morning shadows at the edge of the land
alone, as the waves sifted through the white sand.

All of my cares ebbed away with the tide
as awareness expanded to embrace a world wide;
but as I strolled on the sand, shorter shadows of day
subtly reminded of time passed away.

Lure of the Naiad

Wade knee-deep along the hem
of the lake's scalloped skirt
as toes seek resistance
in the relenting sand.
See my curious minnows
greet you with mouthed O's
as they nudge you invitingly
with timid, welcoming kisses.

Plunge into my watery world…
let its refreshing coolness
massage your body in waves of delight
to shed your tension gradually
from your forehead, shoulders,
and down your legs
in rippling layers,
peeling away your every care.

Marvel at the hazy forms
of magnified shells, pebbles
and polished glass that glow
in liquid-filtered sunlight.

Glide along the weed bank…
laze where lacy green dancers hula
to the rhythm of the waves above,
their undulating skirts
adorned with snail jewels.
Enter into their flowing dance
with limber weightlessness.

Now race the bulging bubbles
toward their element…and
as you shatter the surface
scatter parting gifts
of liquid diamonds.

Nirvana

Diving down

far beneath the surface,

I find a mystical haven

at the vortex of my soul,

where I need no longer breathe,

need not feel, see, nor hear;

for, sensing all, I have no need

for senses. All is known.

Timelessness overcomes space;

and peace replaces need for place.

Levitation

Face, torso, knees and toes
form a chain of islands
in a tranquil, tropical sea
as I float, hands behind my neck,
on the soft, Lake Huron waters,
my chest slowly rising and sinking
to the rhythm of my breathing.

Water presses up from below
as if to reject this land-creature
out of its element;
but I'm content to stay
so as not to chase away
a weightless, lime-green dragonfly
which has mistaken my knee
for a landing stone.

Lacking my extra layer
of feminine fat,
our son, lazing on a tube,
wonders aloud, "How long
could you float like that?"
"Perhaps long enough
to fall asleep," I say,
"on a day like today
with no waves on the way—
long enough to marvel
at this perfect summer day
when time, like my atoll,
seems suspended
in limitless space
in this idyllic place
on the face of this placid,
sun-blessed, blue planet."

Girls' Camp Skinny-Dip

Camp Hanoum, Vermont, 1955

it seemed illogical
to wear our bathing suits
down the wooded path
to the swimming hole
yet once there
we peeled them off
along with our inhibitions
like banana skins
before slipping into
the sun-shimmered waters
that clothed us
like cool satin gowns
fluttering around our legs
as we swam

the wooded hills
above the lake echoed
the delighted squeals
and excited splashes
of even the older campers
and the shoulders
of the newer counselors
rounded to conceal
gradually relaxed
at the realization
that the little dippers
were too wrapped up
in their own delight
to indulge in voyeurism

ah total freedom
from tight leg bands
shoulder straps
and bathing caps
      that trap water
      in the ears
from embarrassment of the fall
from gravity
and one's own body weight

in the calm
of a light evening
the laws of man
and nature paused
allowing a reprieve
of breeze and bugs
restrictions
and busy schedules

the youngest campers
filled the dock-enclosed area
called the "lobster pot"
like a school of
wriggling minnows
only impending darkness
could drive them out
of the slippery waters

back in the clear
shallow waters
of the lobster pot
lurks a memento
of the excitement
symbol of the ultimate freedom
lying like a sea cucumber
on an ocean floor

Inversion Excursion

I'm paddling my kayak upside-down.
    Doesn't everyone from time to time?

Shell and pebble stars dot my sky of sand.
    Like children hanging by their knees
    from swing bars, seaweed
    waves me gleefully along.

From below, light rays filter up
    to spotlight my underchin
    like a child makes a ghoul face
    with a night flashlight.

Glancing down, I am flashed tauntingly
    by white underbellies of fish.

That paddling is next to impossible
    and progress immeasurable
    is immaterial. After a while
    one fish belly looks like another.

Power Glide

Offshore a gentle swell
smoothly lifts my kayak,
bears it gently as a leaf
on its crest before
settling us in the trough,
to anticipate the next
surging wave of power.

Angler

You cast your hopes far out
    and wait, gazing through wavelets,
    which capture your dreams
    and reflect them, magnified.

The mystique of fishing is
    that invisible, unfathomable
    reality that lurks deep
    beneath the imagination.

Wood On Water

She's a sturdy boat.
    (the fisherman said)
Planned her design
    in my very own head.
Build her m'self
    from stem to stern.

Her wood was steamed
    and shaped just right;
her gun'ls are broad;
    and her caulk is tight.
She's stable and true
    when she makes a turn.

She came alive
    at her first taste of water—
Behaves the same
    for m'wife or daughter—
Floats right side up
    in an eight-foot wave.

When the skipper errs,
    she's very forgiving;
she's what makes
    my life worth living—
Love her so much,
    I'd be her slave.

eidolon

from our boat a hazy horizon
almost masks
distant thunderheads

foil-lined wavelets
glint morse code messages
back to the sun

random whitecaps
entice the breeze
to play catch-me-if-you-can

the rise and fall
pitch and yaw
lull the mind
away from its mission

the fishing
was a good excuse
to be here
but let's reel in
and cut the trolling motor

so nothing interrupts
this moment

in my mind
with you

Distant speeding boat
ruffles the horizon line
which soon is becalmed

* * *

The boat's angry wake
shoves it into the harbor
then smugly retreats

* * *

Port Austin Reef Light—
battleship on horizon
defending the rocks

* * *

sky shouts a farewell
sun lingers on horizon
hesitant to leave

Magnetic Sea

The sea intrigues with clouded mystery
of teeming life secretly sequestered,
leaving subtle clues on the shore
as its changing chapters unfold.

When complications threaten creativity
with mind-limiting distractions,
the sea's vast, open range frees imagination
to roam unfenced and unfettered.
Tension of life's pressure subsides
with the rhythmic rocking of the waves,
like a fussy infant calmed
by a gentle, soothing mother.
If I am enervated and weary,
the wildness of its strutting waves
awakens my sluggish brain
and energizes my spirit.
The brilliance of a molten sun,
magnified in elusive reflection,
shatters into darts of light
which disperse brooding moodiness.

Though pinned to earth by gravity,
I am buoyed on the surface of the salty sea—
an ethereal being floating free
in a vision of what I aspire to be.
Like me, the sea is bound to planet earth,
but it glimmers the constantly flowing,
limitless, provident power of God.

Early Morning on the Gulf of Mexico

Fingers of fog rise
from the breeze-speckled
surface of the Gulf waters
to tickle the warm rays
of the early morning sun.

A cormorant floats low
gathering breath
for his next probing dive.
Pelicans await the fortune
that this day will bring.

Inhaling deeply
I, too, savor the potential
of the coming hours.

* * * * * *

No starfish today-
sympathetic waves offer
sand dollar solace

Earth and Water

We are water and earth,
my loved one and I.
I am the water
that flows to the sea;
he is the land mass
to stabilize me.
Oh, what bliss
it is to be
contained in his love,
yet still flowing free!

*   *   *   *   *   *   *   *

After three-day storm
repentant ocean atones
with sand dollar fines

Insight

White sand molds my footprints
as I trudge the green Gulf's rim
searching for its treasures,
straining to discover
that rare, perfect shell.

The beach is clean except
for unseen morsels sought
by sanderlings on toothpick legs.
Yet here a bisected razor clam
displays inner iridescence—
subtle impressionistic colors
displayed posthumously;
and there a broken fragment
reveals a complex labyrinth
concealed in life by outer shell.

The revelation of age is beauty,
of brokenness – insight.

The sparkle of sunlight on water
reflects the fleeting nature
of elusive happiness.
I snatch it with my eyes
and clutch it to my heart,
where it elevates my spirit
and shouts a paeon
to the Creator.

Beachwalk

To seek the clues of life
brought up from the deeper sea...
To read the tracks of those
who passed ahead of me...

To feel the sting of sand,
stand at the edge of land,
and hear the seabirds cry
their calls as they glide by...

To send my thoughts as far
as imagination can propel,
and receive revealing answers
from where the spirit dwells...

To find a pale blue crab
or an exquisite shell ...
To breathe the salty air
and feel my spirits swell...

To see in nature God's awesome power
in mighty waves as well as tiny flower...
My beach walk's so much more
than mere stroll along the shore.

Lesson Learned From My Daughter While Walking the Beach in the Rain in Search of Sea Treasures:

If
you're not
wearing your glasses,
and it looks round
or oblong,
nudge it
with the toe
of your beach shoe
before picking
it up
with your fingers!

* * * * * * * *

Flotsam

On my walk along the beach today
no treasured shells or starfish lay,
but I found poems along the way!

* * * * * * * *

beachcombers match steps
then, having found sea treasures,
break step to catch up

Shopping at the Seashore Sea Store

Shopping the empty beach
before the morning rush of shell seekers,
only one now-fading set
of furtive footprints before me—
this beach is clean; pristine, crystal sand
displays no treasures.
Gulls face the Gulf
as if willing a trust from the sea;
their expectant longing
mirrors my own as I eagerly seek
the perfect Scotch Bonnet shell,
beautiful, with rolled brim
and intricately carved crown.
One mile of vacant beach
produces one blue crab
skeleton with legs dissected;
the eviscerator only a few yards
away, preening and planning
its next feast.
The second mile offers
a lively blue crab
stranded in sink sand.
He raises himself high on tiny legs
and menaces me with tiny pincers.
I goad him into a death grip
on my driftwood stick,
then gently fling him back
to his watery home
to cheat the gulls of one more meal.
The third mile of rhythmic,
arm-swinging march,
triple-timed to match
the pounding surf's cadence,
displays a perfect starfish
placed kindly in my path
as if by a secret benefactor—
compensation from the sea-store
to console me for its
depleted stock of Scotch Bonnets.

Dolphins at Dawn

We come arunning at the shout,
"Dolphins out! Dolphins out!"
hoping to see them dive and spout
as dolphins pass along our way.

Why is it people tend to say,
"We saw the dolphins at their 'play'"?
Is it that they bear a smile
and as they swim away the miles
seem to be playing all the while?

No matter what the people say,
the fun we see is work, not play—
they have to catch a lot of fish
just to fill one dolphin's dish.

* * * * *

As we walk the beach
shy dolphins surface and spout,
echoing our thrill.

The Message

Running at sunset
on the firm-packed sand,
I leave the crowded beach
behind, exulting at
the space and solitude,

running
through wet sink-sand
that tries to slow my pace
to a pensive walk,

running, as waves splash
roaring voices from infinity
toward the dunes,
which absorb and retain
their tantalizing secrets.

As I'm running
horizon flashes
a futile message
from the power of creation;

but I'm running
with hair flying,
salty skin tingle-dried
by the wind,
which whispers hints
into my ears,
which only listen
to the beat
of my feet
running.

Battle For The Beach

Gusts of a northern gale
defend the shore, forcing the waves
of the Gulf's attacking navy
to retreat in confusion.
The few that penetrate the front lines
have their frothy hats blown backwards
in a defiant insult to their ineptitude.
Dwindling breakers scatter in terror
as the invisible horde sweeps down
in a thundering air attack.

Meanwhile, I shiver
from the shrieking whistle
of the blustering army
as we huddle
in our beach cottage.

After fighting waves
beached jellyfish, exhausted,
await the high tide.

* * * * *

silver fish at dawn
glinting on the horizon
hail the golden sun

* * * * *

Toothpick-legs running,
sanderling stops abruptly
to drill for dinner.

* * * * *

clouds at horizon
like alabaster cities
Atlantis revived

O, The Sky!

O, the sky,
the ever-changing sky,
with sea rolling,
rolling far beneath!
This is all the world I need
to make my life complete.
With, of course, some land—
a bit of land beneath my feet.
Oh, yes, and trees...

Like The Wave

Like the wave
that bears the reflection
of the morning sun
toward the shore,
we who love
advance the cause of Goodness
toward fulfillment.

Breaker

I am a wave
urged on by the random winds,
carried along amid other surging waves,
as powerful forces
determine our direction.

Aspirations growing,
I bear birds, boats and flotsam on my way.
I struggle not to cave in to the mounting pressure;
but swelling ever greater,

I finally roll over
with a great, crashing climax
as my being is reduced to froth;
and I float as spindrift,

flat and helpless on a spent sea,
leaving only scattered bits
of beached ocean chaff
as witness to my brief existence.

Ocean Olympics – Finish Line

In a great rush, racing breakers

shove each other forward impatiently,

crash before reaching the finish,

and succumb to the struggle

in a slurry of sand.

Meet the Poet

Jane (Engemann) Mayes lives on the shore of Lake Huron at Port Austin, Michigan, where she drew her inspiration for this collection from the beauty, scope and intricacy of creation. She also expresses her appreciation for nature through watercolor.

Her *raisons d'être* are her husband, three children, two "in-loves" and six grandchildren plus an international village of relatives and friends.

Holding degrees, a B.A. in French and English from Aquinas College and an M.A. in School Librarianship from Central Michigan University, Jane is now retired. She finds that she still reads mostly to learn.

In addition to poetry, art and doing anything with grandchildren, biking, swimming, puddling around in a kayak, reading, golf, and gardening are favorite activities. She and her husband raise Standardbred horses and enjoy seasonal visits to Destin, Florida.

Notes on Poems

"Breathe a Poem," *The Old-Millpond Anthology*. Phil Long, ed, Big Rapids, MI, Autumn 2000.

"The Strike," *The Huron Daily Tribune*. Bad Axe, MI, Oct. 3,2001.

"Territorial Dispute," *Blessed Pests of the Beloved West*. Schnecker Shorb, Yvette and Terril, eds., Native West Press, Prescott, AZ, Oct. 2003, p.84.

"Dark green and lacy," in "Haiku and Related Forms," *Potpourri*. Prairie Village, KS, Vol. 11, No. 2,1999, p.26.

"Love's Yellow Rose," choral music by Kenneth Galbreath, 2003.

"an arrow of geese," in "Haiku and Related Forms," *Potpourri*, Prairie Village, KS, Vol. 11, No. 3,1999.

"Quiescence," *A New Song*. Dayton, OH, Vol. 3, No. 1, Fall/Winter 1997-98; *East of Sunrise*. National Library of Poetry, Owings Mills, MD, 1995.

"Succor," *The Old-Millpond Anthology*. Phil Long, ed., Big Rapids, MI, Spring 2002.

"Affluence Spoken Here," hon. mention, Thumb Area Writers' Club contest, 1992; *A Joyful Noise*. Spiritual Quest, Venice, FL, 1993; *The Old-Millpond Anthology*. Phil Long, ed., Big Rapids, MI, Fall 2001.

"Then Would We?" 2nd place award, Poetry Society of Michigan contest, 2002.

"Filtration," hon. mention, Poetry Society of Michigan contest, Apr.2001.

"Sweetwater Symphony," First prize, Poetry Society of Michigan contest, Aug. 1999; *Peninsula Poets*, Poetry Society of Michigan, Spring 2000.

"current caresses," in "Haiku and Related Forms," *Potpourri*, Prairie Village, KS, Vol. 9, No. 3,1997.

Printed in the United States
34445LVS00006B/88-510

9 781420 855746